FABIAN SOCIETY

CW00369222

The Fabian Society is Britain's leading left of centre think tank and political society, committed to creating the political ideas and policy debates which can shape the future of progressive politics.

With over 300 Fabian MPs, MEPs, Peers, MSPs and AMs, the Society plays an unparalleled role in linking the ability to influence policy debates at the highest level with vigorous grassroots debate among our growing membership of over 7000 people, 70 local branches meeting regularly throughout Britain and a vibrant Young Fabian section organising its own activities. Fabian publications, events and ideas therefore reach and influence a wider audience than those of any comparable think tank. The Society is unique among think tanks in being a thriving, democratically-constituted membership organisation, affiliated to the Labour Party but organisationally and editorially independent.

For over 120 years Fabians have been central to every important renewal and revision of left of centre thinking. The Fabian commitment to open and participatory debate is as important today as ever before as we explore the ideas, politics and policies which will define the next generation of progressive politics in Britain, Europe and around the world.

Fabian Society
11 Dartmouth Street
London SW1H 9BN
www.fabians.org.uk

First published 2007
ISBN 978 0 7163 4104 8

British Library Cataloguing in Publication data. A catalogue
record for this book is available from the British Library.

Printed by Bell & Bain, Glasgow

Labour's Choice

THE DEPUTY LEADERSHIP

Hilary Benn
Hazel Blears
Jon Cruddas
Peter Hain
Harriet Harman
Alan Johnson

Edited by Tom Hampson

CONTENTS

PREFACE

The democratisation of debate has perhaps been the most striking change to British political writing since the Fabian Society began publishing essays and pamphlets over 120 years ago. Policy is debated not only in the newspaper columns of opinionated commentators and in increasingly sophisticated political analysis across the mainstream media but now also online amongst political writers and bloggers across the globe. And – fortunately for us – this swirl of opinion and information has only strengthened the need for the short, cogent and well-argued essay.

This collection of essays is published at a unique moment in the history of the British Labour Party and of the progressive left. The summer of 2007 sees Labour marking an unparalleled ten years in power and this year's leadership elections give us a chance to weigh up Labour's achievements against the tasks left undone.

This is a moment that we must capture and use. And the Fabian Society has long been the forum for these debates. We are the place where the Labour Party – from its leaders to its grassroots – thinks about what matters most to it and about how to turn those beliefs into practical politics, and we are also a bridge between Party members and the broader progressive movement. The modern media age and the experience of opposition means that Labour's leaders are all too aware of the cost of disunity and division. But lack of substantial debate is just as dangerous.

The Fabians have traditionally held hustings for the Labour Party leadership elections and given candidates – from Attlee, Gaitskell and Wilson to Kinnock, Smith and Blair – the opportunity to write essays and set out their stalls. It is important that we have these debates openly, critically and pluralistically. This has long been the Fabian way: we are affiliated to – indeed, we helped to found – the Labour Party and we are proud of it. But it is because we maintain our independence that that we are able to maintain our usefulness. With that in mind, we are currently developing our agenda for the next decade of British politics, focusing on life chances and equality, democracy, the environment, education, and foreign policy.

In this collection, we have asked the candidates for the Deputy Leadership of the Labour Party to write us Fabian Essays that reflect their views on the challenges facing the Government and progressive politics.

We hope that these six authors – all members of the Fabian Society themselves – will help encourage a productive debate about the next decade of British politics.

TH

Hilary Benn is MP for Leeds Central and has been Secretary of State for International Development since 2003.

OUR FUTURE TOGETHER

Hilary Benn

Winning the next election

It is clear that the next election will be the most closely fought in years and that we now face the greatest test of our character for a generation. If just 17,000 people had voted differently in 2005, Labour would not have gained a majority. And while we must continue to work hard in the most marginal seats, we must not be tempted to run a narrow campaign.

Winning the next election will depend on broadening our support, listening to what people have to say, and showing how Labour politics will make a difference in each neighbourhood. And it will depend on building a grassroots party that faces outwards and represents the new kind of politics that I think people want.

We will only renew our Party if we work together. At home, a decade of economic growth and investment in public services is now almost taken for granted. The Tories are more confident, the Liberals, Nationalists and BNP are active in our heartlands and a growing culture of cynicism is undermining our democracy. If this is to be the century in which Labour politics really shapes British public life, we must set a new direction.

We can all look back on the last ten years with pride, but politics is about the future. We live in an age of unprecedented interdependence – with economic globalisation, climate change and new security threats – and of unprecedented potential to defeat poverty and build a better world. Our values and our commitment to social justice will not change. In 1997 we were carried to government on the hope of better things, but in 2007 we must show that we have the confidence and the ideas to take Britain forward once again.

We need to win the trust of the people who voted for us in three elections. So our priorities must be to: show that Labour is the only party that understands the changing world and that will help Britain to change in response; represent a more straightforward kind of politics that listens to people, explains decisions clearly and speaks in a direct, open and personal way; demonstrate that as well as maintaining a strong economy Labour is also strong on the things that will matter most to people at the next election, including public services, (particularly education and the NHS); building strong and safe communities; ensuring that people can afford to find somewhere to live; and tackling climate change.

A more straightforward politics

A more straightforward approach is vital if we are going to reconnect the Party, the leadership and the people, and restore the health of our democracy and trust in our public life. It is also the only way to deal with the corrosive cynicism that pervades too much of our politics.

I am not interested in personality politics or squabbling. I think members and voters are tired of that. I will speak up and speak out for our values, and stand up for a strong Cabinet and collective discussion leading to collective decisions.

Party reform should be an important part of this new politics. I know grassroots members too often feel as if they are on the outside looking in at their own Government through a window. That's why I want to help build a leadership that unites our Party and is trusted by the electorate; one that respects our members and connects the grassroots to the Government.

Our Party needs a sense of excitement again. We joined the Party to change the world, and not to change the minutes of the last meeting. As part of a more straightforward approach, I believe above all that the Party has to look outwards. We need to act on the responsibility we have to help change things, by doing more in, and with, local communities on local issues.

Our Party also needs to restore a sense of partnership. The Labour Party is nothing if not a collective endeavour. We need a frank and more direct relationship between leaders and members, recognising that compromise and negotiation are at the heart of politics. We need to be more open and transparent, and to be unafraid of debate and disagreement. And we need always to remember that the Party is a policy-making body, a social network and a community organisation as well as being an electoral machine.

Confident in what we believe

We have made enormous progress in healing the divided society we were in 1997, but we are not yet content and there is so much more we could do. Nor can we rely on our record or distant memories of boom-and-bust economics, spiralling poverty and chronic under investment under the Tories to win next time. No, to meet the aspirations of a new generation, our vision for Britain's future must be clear.

Our success on the economy and investment in public services, in reducing crime and antisocial behaviour, and in improving education will be the foundation of our future together, but if there is one thing we should also have learned it is that values matter just as much as policies. And values cannot be legislated for; they come from people and how we treat one another, and they have to be nurtured and sustained. So let's be confident in talking about what we believe in and about the kind of society we are trying to build.

I want a country which acts on its concern about poverty, whether in Africa or at home. I want a society that places as much importance on our children and on how we relate to one another as it does on economic stability. I want a politics in which we ask people to give something back, as well as asking things of others. I want a culture which celebrates what people do to contribute, whether in public service, business, or in their local community. I want a Labour Government which doesn't just redistribute wealth, but which also redistributes power and opportunity to make society fairer. I want a world that puts justice and working with others at the heart of our foreign policy.

I know that many of you have these same hopes for the future. In this essay I have set out some of the first steps we could take. This is not intended to be a manifesto; rather, I hope it will be the basis for a discussion and the start of an enduring exchange of ideas.

– A country that acts on its concern about poverty, whether in Africa or at home
I will never forget marching alongside 250,000 people on the streets of Edinburgh in 2005. That summer, more than eight million of us wore a white band to show our support

for the campaign to Make Poverty History and to demonstrate our belief that together – through politics – we could change things.

And we did. That campaign gave leaders the world over the encouragement they needed to make the brave decisions people wanted. And as Secretary of State for International Development, I have seen first hand how much difference we have together made. Children are now in school and people live free from disease, with the chance to make the most of their lives, because of the generosity of spirit and recognition of our common humanity we showed as a nation and a world.

But as MP for Leeds Central – a constituency with one of the highest rates of child poverty – I am only too aware that despite the progress we have made over the last decade in fighting poverty in Britain, we have so much more to do. What really links poverty and disadvantage here and in the developing world is wasted human potential.

It is simply unacceptable that in the fifth richest country in the world, more than 3.6 million adults and 3.4 million children live in poverty in our towns, cities and countryside. A quarter of the poorest families in Britain say they can't afford to have their friends or family round for a meal at least once a month. Women earn less than men for the same day's work. And if you are born in Bethnal Green you will die 15 years earlier than if you are born in Chelsea.

Changing this is not a question of ability. It is a question of political support and political will.

– A society that places as much importance on our children and on how we relate to one another as it does on economic stability

A stable economy has been the bedrock of our success over the last decade. But it isn't everything. While tackling poverty and inequality must remain at the heart of what we do, what makes each of us happy – and what we look forward to most – is more than just the next pay cheque or pay rise, important though they are. It's also about making a contribution to society, spending time with each other, and seeing our children grow up healthy and fulfilled.

We have done a huge amount to improve children's and families' lives since 1997. 600,000 fewer children live in poverty, and millions of parents benefit from extended maternity and paternity leave and increased pay. Yet children from the poorest families are today still six times less likely to pass five GCSEs than their better off counterparts and five times more likely to die in a road accident. And one in seven of our young people have mental health problems.

At the next election, it will be more important than ever for us to build on the foundations of the strong economy we have created and the reforms we have put in to improve our families' and children's lives. The Tories talk of social responsibility, but they forget that the state too has a responsibility to offer a helping hand.

Investing in our families and our children is without doubt the best way to improve our society. Sure Start, extended maternity and paternity leave and pay reforms are important achievements. But we must go further.

– A politics in which we ask people to give something back, as well as asking things of others
The 'me first', go-it-alone culture of the 1980s and early 1990s did untold damage to our communities, public services and families, and we are still feeling the effects. No society can prosper if it neglects to nurture the value of putting something back.

Although we cannot legislate for community spirit, or pass a law to say that young people should support each other in school or that we should look out for our neighbours, we should not simply shrug our shoulders and say we cannot influence the values of our society.

These do have to come partly from within and we should ask people to contribute to shaping them. For without these values there is something missing from society. But government also has a role. Investing in public services and in communities, offering a helping hand to those who make an effort, and supporting and defending unions, the voluntary sector and the public service ethos all make a difference.

I worry that if we don't say this – and act on it – then consumerist politics will take over. Politics is not the same as shopping. We did not change things in the past by sitting back and expecting someone else to do it, and we won't overcome the challenges of the future without people playing their part.

– A culture which celebrates what people do to contribute, whether in public service, business, or in their local community

We are very bad at recognising and celebrating what people contribute and do well. We read all the time about the things that have gone wrong. It's important that we do acknowledge these because it keeps us on our toes and leads to important reforms, but it does also mean that we hold up a distorted mirror to ourselves as a society.

And yet it is a remarkable feature of modern Britain that people's personal experience of public services is by and large hugely positive, while their perception of the national picture is less so. If you ask people about whether they were treated well on their last visit to a hospital, about four in five say they were. But if you ask them about whether the NHS is providing a good service nationally, just half say it is. A question: why don't people trust their own experience more?

And as I work in my constituency and travel the country and the world, I am more than anything else struck by the number of people who give their time and their talent to helping others in community groups, trade unions and civil society. Another question: why don't we celebrate this more?

So as we have transformed the politics of investment in public services, our aim for the next decade should be to transform the politics of public life more broadly.

– A Labour Government which doesn't just redistribute wealth, but which also redistributes power and opportunity to make society fairer

My time working for a union and in local government taught me what it means to be on the frontline for Labour – particularly as chair of the education committee and as Deputy Leader of Ealing Council in the years where local democracy was assaulted by the Tories and undermined by cuts to the budgets and powers of councils.

But more than that, it taught me that if you want people to make the best of themselves then you should give them responsibility. And I hope we can use this election to make the case for strong local government that gives local communities the power to do things for themselves.

It is the way both to match people's rising expectations about life and about public services – we are a better educated, less deferential society and that is a good thing – with the responsibility we must all accept to play our part. It is also the way to help us come to terms with globalisation by showing that there are decisions we can take and influence locally; for example, how we are policed, how we deal with anti-social behaviour and how our local community is run.

Achieving social justice in the 21st century will depend on more than just redistributing wealth. It will also require us to redistribute power and opportunity to make society fairer.

– A world that puts justice and working with others at the heart of our foreign policy

I think we are at a turning point for our world. If the 20th century was defined by the ideological conflict that began with the Russian revolution and ended with the collapse of the Berlin wall, then this century will be shaped by a different choice: between a world that looks outwards, embraces multilateralism and seeks to shape globalisation in the interests of social justice – on the one hand – or a world in which isolationism, protectionism and narrow nationalism hold sway – on the other.

As nation states we need to decide. Do we pursue our narrow short-term national interest? Do we turn in on ourselves? Or do we face this new world of ours with confidence, recognising that our national interest is now inextricably tied to the global interest and to the development of nations. Can we fashion the international arrangements that will manage our differences and create the peace and security that is the dream of every single one of us?

All the big challenges we face – overcoming climate change, making the world trade rules fairer, fighting global poverty and dealing with threats to our security – will depend on us working together. What do we do when states or those within states commit crimes against humanity? That's why we need a multilateral system that works. And the more we can show it does, the stronger our argument – with those who would act unilaterally – that there is another way.

As we look to the future, I think the answer to these questions must lie in putting a renewed commitment to justice and to working with others at the heart of our foreign policy.

Our potential

This is a moment of truth for us all. What we decide to do as a Party will have an impact far beyond our membership. It will help shape the world we live in. It is why politics matters. It's why Labour politics changes people's lives.

It's also why this election matters. It is about our future together. I hope you will take part and, whatever the outcome, I look forward to working with you over the months and years ahead.

*Hazel Blears is MP for Salford, Minister
without Portfolio and Party Chair. She was
previously a Home Office Minister and
Public Health Minister.*

BUILDING ON SUCCESS

Hazel Blears

It is right that this collection of essays is titled 'Labour's Choice'. The choice before us is far more significant than who gets what job at the top of the Party. This is a pivotal moment in the Party's history, when we make a choice about the fundamental position and trajectory of our Party. We are the first generation of Labour activists to be choosing a Leader and Deputy Leader when the Party is in government. It is a weighty responsibility.

Two paths

There are two paths that we can follow. The first is to retreat into our Labour comfort zone, play the old tunes and contribute to a sense that New Labour was a distasteful (albeit successful) electoral ploy, whose time has been and gone. This retreat merely plays into our opponents' myth-making that Labour's majorities were an historic aberration, carried on the shoulders of a leadership which is departing the stage.

This course also fails to understand the true nature of New Labour. The deep-seated reconnection that the Party made with the electorate in the mid-90s was rooted in a modern definition of our traditional values. It was not an denial of our socialism, rather it was its restatement in tune with modern times and modern society. If we understand our past successes in this context, as a process of applying socialist values to contemporary concerns and aspirations, then we can equip ourselves with a governing strategy which transcends individual leaders and transitory events.

The second path, then, is to build on Labour's past successes, to be proud of what we have achieved in a decade of Labour Government, and to have the confidence that we can go on to further success. A few years ago I was attacked by the right wing press for daring to suggest that Labour could be in office for decades, not just years. It was suggested that this was arrogant or even out of touch.

Yet there is no iron law of politics which says that the Tories must win elections and that Labour must lose them. If Labour can construct a political platform which commands support from a broad enough coalition of the electorate, then there is no logical reason why we cannot witness a century characterised by social progress led by Labour in government.

If we are confident that our values are the people's values, that our policies are both popular and right, then we should have the self-belief to want our Party to enjoy a sustained period in office. I've described it elsewhere as the 'governing gene' and we have to prove that we still have it.

More of the same?
But when I say that we should build on our success, it is mischievous to suggest that this simply means 'more of the same'. None of the candidates in this election want 'more of the same' because we all understand that times change, society changes, and the threats and opportunities we face change too.

It is obvious that some of the challenges we face over the coming decade are different from the challenges we faced in the past. The political landscape in April 1997 was very different: mass unemployment, record house repossessions and business failures, and not a single woman in the Cabinet.

Today, we face environmental, technological and societal changes on a scale that we couldn't foresee in 1997. Just consider the way the Internet – in its infancy in 1997 – has transformed the way we work, shop, and run our lives. Or the explosion of digital technology. Or advances in gene therapy and micro-surgery. Or the growth of concern about climate change. Or global terrorism. Or even just the ways we use our mobile phones today compared to a decade ago.

These changes generate insecurity and unease for some. They also create huge shifts in aspirations and expectations, and any successful progressive government must anticipate and meet these contradictory moods of apprehension and aspiration. Labour must be the party of aspiration and success.

Staying on the centre ground

Crucial to our policy-formulation is the need to remain camped firmly on the centre ground of British politics. We cannot win an election by appealing only to a few hundred thousand Labour members and trade unionists. When we've retrenched into our heartlands in the past, the people living in those heartlands got clobbered by Conservative Governments.

The only reason people in Salford got jobs, a minimum wage and new school buildings is because people in Swindon, Sittingbourne and South Dorset voted Labour. Our instinctive support for the poorest and most vulnerable must be tempered by the need to win elections. The poorest people in our communities don't want our solidarity and sympathy; they want the practical means to stop being poor. And that starts with a Labour Government.

The policy challenges

Let's turn to some of the policy areas that I would identify as being the most pressing. Our starting point must be the economy. We cannot achieve anything against the backdrop of a faltering or failing economy. So we must build on our economic success. Every past Labour Government failed ultimately because of economic failure. Every time we lost an election, it was because the Tories could claim that Labour was economically reckless or incompetent. What New Labour achieved in the mid-90s was the formulation that not only was economic efficiency compatible with social justice, but that one was reliant on the other.

Fabians may remember Gordon Brown's important Fabian pamphlet *Fair is Efficient* in April 1994, which set out the case. In government, that theory has become practice. By tackling unemployment and creating two million extra jobs, we have created a more efficient economy. Millions of families are now free from the blight of unemployment, men and women have the fulfilment and independence that comes from work, and millions more children are growing up seeing their parents going out to work in the morning. But as well as the positive impact that employment has on individual lives and communities, it is better for the economy.

Gordon Brown has managed a seismic shift from wasting money on unemployment benefit to investing in public services – £5 billion a year. By reducing the national debt, we have saved £4 billion a year. By creating a stable framework of low interest rates, low inflation and steady growth, we have enabled families and businesses to invest, prosper, and plan ahead with confidence.

But our movement towards full employment creates its own tensions. So in the next ten years we must address the work-life balance, the problems of commuting and the opportunities for home working, and the need for more flexibility for parents, carers and disabled people.

This economic success must provide the platform for greater efficiency and greater fairness over the coming decade.

– We must be on the side of aspirant families.

Ernie Bevin said, "It's inherent in the working class to want a better deal for your children than your parents or grandparents had." That remains true today, and when Labour has been in touch with people's aspirations as in 1945 and 1997, we win. When we fail to key into this aspiration, for example in the early 80s when we failed to back people's desire to own their council house, we divorce ourselves from the people.

Take housing. I believe that housing is as big an issue today as it was in 1945. Then, the issue was a massive shortage of housing. Today, the problems are multi-faceted. First-time buyers and key workers are priced out of the market in most parts of the country.

Different generations of families are split when young families cannot afford to live near their parents. We are not building enough affordable decent homes for single people.

I would seek an end to ideological divides on housing policy, and allow local stakeholders including housing associations and local authorities to agree a local housing plan and plan their repairs and building programme based on local communities' needs.

I would encourage more housing co-ops and shared equity schemes. We also need to ensure that investors do not buy properties in hot spots but deliberately leave them vacant.

When it comes to housing, what matters is what works. I welcome stricter regulations on the estate agency business, with a stronger voice for consumers. But we also need a new form of local community-owned estate agency which is run as a social enterprise, with profits recycled into community benefits such as energy efficiency. I intend to meet with the Co-op to discuss this idea.

We need to learn from the success of schemes such as the Urban Splash redevelopment in Salford where traditional terraced houses have been turned into fashionable urban homes, and from the transformation of our city centres where more people are living than ever before.

– We must tackle persistent pockets of poverty.
The only sustainable route out of poverty is work, so full employment must be our goal. No-one should be reliant on benefits; our system of benefits and tax credits should be a ladder out of poverty, not a way of life.

So we need to create a full employment economy in every part of the country, and ensure that every person who is capable of work is in work. This should be done with incentives where possible, and compulsion where necessary.

– Democratic public services
People want more and more from their public services. We need to step up reforms which pass more power to users. People want choice and voice in their schools, health services, transport system and local services.

Take the NHS. We need a renewed effort to engage people in their local health service. It cannot be left to managers and clinicians, no matter how enlightened. The experience of NHS Foundation Trusts has been salutary. Half a million people now belong to NHS Foundation Trusts, and have a say over their running and direction. This should be spread across the NHS.

It is time for a debate on whether there should be a directly-elected element of primary care trusts (PCTs) to allow local accountability and control over local health services.

I would like to see more public ownership within the NHS, for example fewer GPs' and dentists' practices run as private businesses and more as co-ops and mutuals, along the Croydoc model, or with ownership by local communities.

As Deputy Leader I will press for a national celebration to mark the sixtieth anniversary in 2008 of the founding of the NHS every bit as salient as the bicentenary of the act abolishing the slave trade.

– Putting communities in control

Within British socialism there has always existed a strong strand of localism, standing in contrast with the statism of the post-war governments. This older tradition, rooted in the early trade unions, co-ops, friendly societies, guild socialism and women's organisations, has much to teach us today. In small, local organisations real citizenship can be taught and real democracy exercised.

In my Fabian pamphlet *Communities in Control* (2003) I advocated a shift towards community ownership of local assets and services, from local libraries and parks to recycling schemes and Sure Start centres.

Take an issue like climate change. I applaud the Government's efforts to tackle climate change, and welcome individuals' and companies' efforts to cut emissions and waste. But there is a proper community-level response which needs to be co-ordinated, with community action to identify the 'community carbon footprint' and concerted neighbourhood action to reduce it. This opens an intermediate market for local social enterprises, campaigns and social enterprises such as community heat and power schemes.

As Deputy Leader I would challenge the traditional social democratic insistence that the big state is best, and unleash the creative potential of local working class communities to direct, control and own a greater proportion of their amenities and services. This will transform the relationship between citizen and state, and create a new range of organisations where people can develop their potential as community champions and leaders.

– The rebirth of politics

The greatest challenge for the Deputy Leader is the revitalisation of our Party and our politics. The Labour Party cannot carry on as it is. Our relentless cycle of meetings reporting to other meetings saps our energy and wears out our activists. We need to turn the Labour Party outwards to the community, and encourage more campaigning and contact with the electorate. Local Labour Parties should be catalysts for change: cleaning up parks, tackling graffiti and litter, even running local facilities like drop in centres and advice services.

We mustn't throw the baby out with the bath water. We need local structures to select candidates, hold representatives to account, and to discuss policy. But we also need local parties which can attract a range of people who do not want to go to meetings, who use email and Facebook, and who work long hours but still want to give us their support.

Unless we re-engineer our Party, we won't have a national Labour Party in ten years' time, so as Deputy Leader this would be a pressing priority. Our leadership elections must be the start of a rebuilding of our Party membership, and we must emerge from the process stronger than before.

I would introduce a new 'compact' between Labour's elected representatives at all levels and their local Labour parties, agreed locally, to guarantee minimum levels of campaigning and activity. I am also attracted to the Swedish socialists' system of 'party days' when senior party figures including ministers must donate a set number of days a year to purely party campaigning.

We must continue to make advances on the diversity of Labour's candidates and representatives, so that our democratic bodies reflect our communities and society. Political education, training, mentoring, online support and 'headhunting' potential candidates will all play a role in this.

The rebirth of our Party is a prerequisite to the rebirth of politics. I want to see politics returned as a reputable and honourable activity. Let's start with the schools and teach citizenship in ways which rehabilitates party politics. Let's open our parliament to visitors and build a visitors' centre for our citizens not just for tourists. Let's allow party appointments onto public bodies, so being active in party politics is no longer a barrier to public service. We should use any future state funding of parties to encourage local activity, political education and campaigning.

Proud but not satisfied

The Swedish socialists have as their slogan 'proud but not satisfied.'

I too am proud about what we've achieved together. I walk around Salford every week and can see the improvements over the past decade, which the Tories would reverse in the blink of an eye. But I am not satisfied. The job is not finished. Like most Labour activists, I am ambitious for more reforms and improvements, restless for change. One pensioner in poverty is one too many. One family destroyed by crime shames us all.

We need to win the next election, and that can only be done by winning a raft of seats with majorities under a thousand, or even under a hundred. They are clustered around outer London, along the north Kent and south coasts, and in the

Midlands, as well as pockets of the north, Wales and Scotland. These must be our focus, because unless we can convince people here, the Tories will win.

In the coming weeks Labour has the choice: forward or retreat; reaching out, or turning inwards. More of the same is no solution, and neither is a lurch to the left. In the coming months, we have an historic opportunity to renew ourselves in office, and if we can, then future generations will have cause to thank us.

If we fail, it is the most vulnerable people in our communities who will suffer the most.

Jon Cruddas is MP for Dagenham. He worked previously as Assistant to the Labour Party General Secretary and as Deputy Political Secretary to the Prime Minister.

AFTER NEW LABOUR

Jon Cruddas

The coalition built by New Labour is fracturing. Most notably, empirically, it is working class voters that have shown a greater disaffection with New Labour since 1997. Yet discussion of class remains deeply unfashionable in debates about either our organisation, our philosophy or our policy within the Labour Party. This has to change in order to rebuild a wide and deep political movement.

By contrast, portrayals of the working class permeate popular culture, albeit caricatured in comedy or demonised in the debate about crime and anti-social behaviour. Arguably, the cumulative effect of this is that the working class itself has been de-humanised – now to be feared and simultaneously served up as entertainment.

Too often the Labour Government has colluded in this process through its own retreat from class for perceived electoral advantage. This disengagement is hardly ever dissected or even discussed within the Party itself.

This state of affairs stands in contrast to the historic role of the Labour Party as the emancipatory vehicle for the working class. So the question remains: is what is offered up by

New Labour – in its retreat from class – a necessary prerequisite for a modern social democratic revisionism?

I would pose the apparently heretical view that a return to consideration of contemporary class relations and inequality would actually provide for a more durable Labour Government. It would allow us to rebuild a coalition to achieve future electoral successes. To do this we must first understand the fracture of the New Labour coalition.

Critiques and origins of New Labour

The common criticism of New Labour from the left is that it is too conservative. In essence, New Labour is no different from, and therefore part of, the neo-liberal right. This thesis assumes that New Labour has accepted the neo-liberal framework and indeed developed this project through the commodification of public services, the renunciation of redistribution as an act of public policy, its deference to corporate power, its privatisations and the rest.

An alternative take on New Labour is not to assume it is the product of a body of ideas as such. This approach is to see it as primarily driven by the imperatives of power retention. That is, to see it as the pure logical manifestation of Schumpeter's famous dictum that the core of democracy lies in the 'competitive struggle for the people's vote' in a similar form that the capitalist seeks to exchange commodities in the marketplace. In this model votes are the form of exchange; policies are the commodities themselves; and elected office is the derived profit.

We do not, therefore, see New Labour as a consequential product of a series of philosophical positions but rather as a political organisation calibrated for the purpose of winning elections. Ideas or traditions of thought are only introduced to render intelligible this exercise in political positioning. Under this approach, the originality – indeed the genius – of

New Labour rests in the method by which policy is scientifically constructed out of the preferences and prejudices of the swing voter in the swing seat. Policy is the product of positioning, devised through the rigour of polling rather than the rigour of thought.

Class, New Labour and the knowledge economy

Throughout the 1980s and 1990s Labour's problems were seen as being associated with failed periods of economic intervention, tax and spend welfarism and union militancy. The defeat of 1992 pushed policy further towards an active 'supply side socialism' so as to deal with these polling negatives. This trend intensified with the election of Tony Blair.

Polling increasingly determined policy; policy became an exercise in abstract political positioning driven by the demands of swing voters. A few key ideologists rose to the task and sought to make sense of Blairite repositioning with reference to a supposed revolution in economic relations luckily occurring just as Blair became Leader.

Most important in the period 1994-97 was the introduction of a new economic and social world view based around the notion of the 'new knowledge-based economy'. This body of ideas became the axis for New Labour repositioning from 1994 and can still be detected today in the core wiring of the whole New Labour project. Within this framework, globalisation and new information technologies are widely cited as the key contemporary levers of change in work and employment relations.

Future economic prosperity will be driven by the expanding production of knowledge and intangible assets, set against the steady erosion of traditional manufacturing and heavy industry. We assume a rapid growth in scientific, technical, managerial and professional employment and a corresponding decline in traditional manual work, with the distinction between employer and worker gradually eroded. Trade unions and other allegedly rigid institutions must adapt or die, for there is no place in the 'new economy' for traditional, adversarial industrial relations.

For elements within the Labour Party this analysis of the world of work resolved the historic dilemma inherent in previous Labour Governments' support for manufacturing, as supporting this sector offers diminishing returns. It reinforced, intellectually, an in-built hostility to organised labour and labour market regulation from within the Labour Government. Economic policy becomes re-focused on market (and government) failure in the provision of human capital – captured in the famous focus on 'education, education, education'.

These ideas legitimised the repositioning of New Labour into the mythical, classless knowledge economy of middle England. As such, New Labour is free from a working class which is literally withering away. Class, inequality and issues of power can be overcome by individual self-actualisation once we overcome the only inequality that matters – access to human capital. What occurs – for the sake of political positioning – is that the fundamental economic issues that have preoccupied the left for generations are reduced to issues of deficient information and orthodox human capital theory.

The withering of the working class?
For the architects of the 'new knowledge economy' – and as a direct consequence for the underpinning of the electoral positioning of New Labour – there remains one basic problem – empirical evidence for the withering away of the working class.

Manual workers still account for a relatively stable 10.5 million workers – approaching 40 per cent of total employment. If you were to add in clerical and secretarial work then the traditional labour force stands at some 15 million –

approaching two in three jobs. Where are the growth areas in the economy? There has been a slight rise in computer managers, software engineers and programmers but the real growth has been in the long-established services of sales assistants, data input clerks, store keepers, receptionists, security guards and the like.

Alongside this has been a massive expansion in cleaning and support workers in the service sector, and increased work among the caring occupations – for example care assistants, welfare and community workers and nursery nurses. In short, throughout the last fifteen years there has been no revolution in the demand for labour – rather the key growth areas have been in traditional, often low paid, jobs, many of which are carried out by women. What stands out is the emergence of an 'hour glass' economy in the UK. On the top half of the hour glass there has been an increase in high paid jobs, performed by those with significant discretion over their hours and patterns of work – in a generalised sense these might be described as knowledge workers. However, in the UK, of more empirical significance has been the trend growth of low paid, routine and much unskilled work in occupations pre-eminent 50 years ago.

Government analysis presumes that future demand for labour is almost entirely driven by high wage, high skilled, knowledge labour. This is the economic framework upon which it has repositioned the Party and forged its policy agenda. But this approach is at best empirically questionable.

While this may play well for certain pivotal elements within the electorate, it further dislocates the policy process from the empirical realities of modern Britain.

The preceding analysis exposes a real problem for the architects of New Labour which is increasingly being played out in terms of contemporary policy conflicts within the Party and electoral unpopularity. On the one hand, we see a policy-making process that is driven by the preferences and prejudices of swing voters codified increasingly with reference to conservative intellectual traditions and, on the other, the empirical realities of modern Britain, which demand an alternative set of policies in order to confront inequality- in terms of housing, labour market insecurity, patterns of inward migration and the demand for labour and access to public services and the like.

Perhaps the most obvious example of this problem is in the current debate around the efficient allocative properties of markets and the reform of health and education policy. The language of choice is used because of the traction it creates among swing voters. Policy is then built around these buzz phrases with reference to rational choice analysis developed by marginalist theories of efficient exchange – in education around the form of parent power, in health around patient choice.

This deeply ideological agenda is disguised as a progressive devolution of power down to the working class in order to placate internal concerns. This is an exact replica of the form by which neo-classical economics scientifically defines the brilliance of the market. In essence these policies contain the same fundamental weaknesses as the neo-classical framework that has produced them – assumptions of perfect information; the psychology of rational choice and the way an economic subject discounts for the future; the empirical realities of class, race and inequality; the role of intermediary institutions and market imperfection; and so on.

Further tensions emerge when we try and make sense of people's involuntary inactivity or indeed their lack of opportunity. Within the right wing neoclassical frame of reference these remain elusive concepts – beyond the explanatory power of the framework. Either people do not understand their own preferences or fall foul due to imperfect information. We tend to reduce our approach to one of providing fresh incentives or compulsions on those who are often the victims of broader economic and political forces. It is a short hop to actually blaming the victim for their own predicament – again an element in current debate around work, leisure and welfare.

The electoral consequences of New Labour's preoccupation with mythical 'middle England'

It used to be a common observation that New Labour was efficient at winning elections due to its ruthless scientific analysis of the preferences and prejudices of the swing voter in the swing seat and our key seat organisation. Yet this is brought into question as our coalition has fractured. It is another common observation that many working class people are rendered invisible by the current political system – they appear to have no voice. When we even acknowledge the existence of a working class it tends to be demonised – in almost the exact parallel to that of the migrant – so as to reproduce the political power of New Labour within its middle England marketplace. I would suggest that this fracture of the coalition is critically linked to the way we have literally dis-invented a working class – they have been written out of the script as we bet the ranch on a revolution in economic relations.

In order to achieve our preoccupation with certain voters our intellectual world view has been specifically constructed to prioritise their needs whilst simultaneously assuming the withering away of the working class. It is therefore no surprise that we have failed to deal with the material concerns of the latter. It is therefore no surprise to learn that working class voters have had a greater propensity to stop voting Labour compared to any other socio-economic groups since 1997.

The genius of New Labour lay in the broad electoral coalition that swept it to power in 1997; its fracture ten years on should alert us of the need to rebuild this coalition.

New Labour's big tent has gradually shrunk since 1997 and, by 2007, has all but collapsed. A decade ago approximately 15 million people identified themselves with Labour in opinion polls and 14 million of those voted for New Labour in 1997.

By 2005 less than ten million Labour identifiers voted for the Party and another five million natural Labour supporters, people who said they were Labour, either stayed at home or voted for largely non-Tory political alternatives. Hence the analysis that New Labour won in 2005 because of an even more disastrous performance by the Tory Party which managed to poll even fewer votes than it had in 1997.

New survey data of those Labour identifiers who voted for the Party in 2005 reveal even more worrying developments in the abandonment of New Labour. Less than half (45 per cent) said they were enthused by its' policies and over half (53 per cent) said they wanted to see Labour punished with a reduced majority. Those who stayed true to New Labour in 2005 did so because they wanted to stop the Tories and saw no other political alternative.

Careful examination of the 2005 general election results show that those sectors of the electorate who had shown the greatest propensity to vote New Labour just eight years before, were now the most likely to abstain. Scrutiny of the polling data reveals the only social grouping that stayed loyal to New Labour were the professional, administrative and executive classes – those that tend to inhabit the new knowledge economy. Every other social group recorded significant swings away from New Labour.

Every other part of New Labour's core coalition had begun to defect by 2005. The urban intellectuals, the manual working classes in Labour heartland areas, the Black and Minority Ethnic groups and the public sector workers. The rich coalition of social strata which delivered New Labour to a resounding victory in 1997 had moved decisively away from us by 2005. The task at hand is to rebuild across these parts of our coalition.

In 2005 up to 1.25 million people who had previously voted New Labour defected to the Lib Dems – the war in Iraq was central to this. Thousands more cast their votes elsewhere – the SNP, Plaid Cymru and the BNP. Millions more former New Labour voters stayed at home.

In short, New Labour would have been defeated in 2005 had the Tories provided a credible alternative. David Cameron's re-positioning of a 'New' resurgent Tory Party, also camped in the consensual middle ground means we cannot assume the same advantage at the next election.

My hypothesis is, then, that New Labour, as defined by the electoral coalition on which it is founded, is unlikely to win power again and so an urgent change of direction is needed, based on a thorough understanding of Britain as it is now, to build a new basis and firmer foundation for broader electoral support. Central to this is an understanding of class and insecurity at the work place.

The other thing that is evident from the electoral data is that there is room for repositioning to the left of New Labour. This would make Labour more electable. One in five – three million people – who helped deliver New Labour to power in 1997 voted Liberal Democrat in 2005, a party with arguably a more left wing manifesto than New Labour. That group included a range as broad as the one that had previously characterised the New Labour coalition, encapsulating people in the upper middle classes through to manual workers.

Ministers cling to the rhetoric that only the politics of unremitting New Labour will keep Labour in power but this is based on an outmoded assessment of Britain in the 1990s and the hard empirical analysis of the collapse of our electoral coalition.

Some ideologues within the leadership have argued that the key to the next election is maintaining the support of the aspirational middle and upper middle class and, while it is true that their support is necessary, it is not a sufficient condition for victory. If we maintain their support but fail to motivate the rest of our core vote, then we will lose. As an example, the public sector workers' vote alone is worth more than the narrow majorities in dozens of the most marginal seats in the country.

We urgently need to understand why it is that we invested more money in our public services than any Government post war, and yet lost the support of this critical and traditionally core supporting group. The same argument can be applied to people who live in the rented sector housing, as well as to manual workers more generally.

The political demographics are stacking up against New Labour. Historically key supporting groups have deserted the Party and, unless we win these groups back, Labour faces defeat at the next election.

The key to a future victory is to reanimate Labour's lost millions and to mobilise them on the basis of a new progressive consensus, whilst not losing the support of crucial middle class votes.

There is one very important source of hope. This is the fact that – in addition to the almost ten million who voted for us in 2001 – there remained millions more in 2005 who, although they did not vote for us, still identify with Labour values. We have to reanimate these defecting social strata based on a new political consensus.

New Labour was a work of political brilliance and commanded an unprecedented electoral plurality but it was of, and has had, its' time. As others have said, it is no longer 'New' or 'Labour'.

The objective now is to build a modern New Labour project grounded in the realities of the modern world and not some stylised construction of modernity – the new knowledge economy – that scientifically seeks to entrench class and income inequality. This is the challenge for the modernisation of the Party and the overhaul of the policy programme of our movement.

Peter Hain is MP for Neath and Secretary of State for Northern Ireland and for Wales.

RECONNECT TO WIN

Peter Hain

Ten years ago, Labour was swept to power by a broad-based coalition on a promise of radical change. After eighteen years of cramped ambitions and rampant individualism, we offered a compelling vision of the country's future which resonated with most voters. It was one inspired by our Party's enduring belief that 'by the strength of our common endeavour we achieve more than we achieve alone'.

The British people responded with a strong endorsement for a manifesto which was unremittingly radical: the pledge to enact a national minimum wage and end poverty pay; dynamic investment in decaying public services; the promise of full employment; an end to boom and bust; and an historic programme of devolution and constitutional reform.

We won't win a fourth term in government unless we once again offer a radical vision for the future. Only such a vision can, as it did in 1997, reunite a progressive coalition of all parts of the country and all sections to society behind Labour. And only such a coalition is capable of sustaining lasting progressive change.

Indeed, thanks to the progressive promise of 1997, and the broad electoral coalition it inspired, we have succeeded in fundamentally reshaping the British political landscape. On issue after issue where the Conservatives opposed us a decade ago – on the minimum wage; investment in public services; and ending discrimination and ensuring equal rights for all – the Conservatives have now finally admitted that we were right, and they were wrong.

So, we have managed, not simply to occupy the centre ground, but to shift it, fundamentally and irrevocably, to the left. We have built a national consensus around a progressive agenda (in our case economic efficiency, social justice and democracy), just as Labour Governments did with the creation of the NHS in the 1940s, the expansion of higher education in the 1960s or the drive to stamp out discrimination in the 1970s, which could only be overturned by the right at huge political cost.

But ten years into government, it is absolutely essential we recognise that successful centre-left parties only remain in government if they are willing to renew in government. And real renewal (not synthetic renewal) requires us to have an open and honest debate about the new ideas that we'll need to meet the challenges of this young century.

That's why it is vital that we must neither lurch back to a failed old agenda, nor pretend that simply more of the same will be enough to secure us victory at the next election. Both those arguments are being put in the Deputy Leader campaign and both risk defeat.

I strongly believe in a quite different approach. We must retain and build upon the best of our achievements – especially Gordon Brown's management of the economy and public service investment. We must never, as happened with Al Gore in the 2000 American presidential election, appear to turn our backs on the many successes of the last ten years of Labour government under Tony Blair. But we must also adopt a fresh vision to tackle the major challenges of the future.

This will require a much greater push to devolve power out of Whitehall to local communities and individuals; closing the inequality gap; forging a radical red-green agenda to meet the challenge of climate change; whilst being uncompromising about security and safety, jealously guarding liberty; and pursuing a new progressive internationalism to reflect the increasingly interdependent world in which we now live.

And real renewal is crucial if we are to reconnect Labour's leadership with the grassroots, back bench MPs and the trade unions. We have lost touch – especially with the progressive coalition which underpinned our landslide victories in 1997 and 2001. We have lectured too much and listened too little. We have bounced policies on the Party and the country rather than developed policies in consultation with members and citizens.

Some suggest that we should concentrate our efforts simply on appealing to target groups of voters in a small number of marginal seats. But Labour voters exist in all seats – both heartlands and marginals, obviously very much more of them in the former, but still significant enough numbers in the latter to make it essential that they turn out to vote for us. We cannot win without the 'New Labour' voters we attracted in 1997 and held in 2001, but neither can we win without enthusing traditional Labour voters as well. Some seem to have forgotten the real lesson of 1997, which was that we made a successful appeal to voters right across the country, in both heartland Labour seats and 'Middle Britain' constituencies. My majority in the former South Wales mining constituency of Neath was the biggest ever in history; but we also won seats in the South East of England nobody ever dreamt we would.

Our message then was not a narrow appeal to the self-interest of a few thousand voters, but a broad one which emphasised how collective action on behalf of all was to the benefit of each. It must be so again.

The arrival of David Cameron as Tory leader makes such an approach even more critical. Showing the extent to which we have shifted the centre of gravity of British politics, the Tories are now frightened to talk about the very right-wing ideas that, only a few years ago, they claimed as articles of faith, and which Cameron himself drafted into their 2005 manifesto. Instead of attacking our legacy, they pose as our heirs.

Such Tory sophistry must not, however, be allowed to camouflage the underlying and very deep clash of ideas that remains. Over the past ten years, Labour has shown consistently the power of its fundamental belief: that government, as the ultimate expression of the collective will of individual citizens, can and should be a force for realising the good society we are trying to build. Progressives, as Bill Clinton put it, are those willing to engage in 'the relentless search for the common good'.

But while the Tories are now giving the impression of being reconciled to an active, progressive government, their current blueprint for a 'hollowed-out state' – with tax cuts for the few, contracted-out services for the many and huge cuts in Labour's public investment plans – simply reflects their enduring hostility to government. By attempting to 'sub-contract' all responsibility for the social needs of our poorest communities to 'the people themselves', the mission of 'Cameronism' is clear: to cloak in the velvet glove of compassion the traditional conservative fist of minimal government.

But we must do more than simply reveal the Tories' true intentions. As they seek to claim – however disingenuously – our progressive mantle, we must reinforce our right to it.

This will require us to be clearer about the kind of government we want.

We must beware of the false choice that the Tory leader is attempting to erect: between 'big' or 'nanny' government on the one side and their vision of a 'limited state' on the other. The real choice is between our belief that government can be part of the solution to the problems which citizens face in an uncertain world and the Tories' belief that government is the problem. We must advance our Labour vision of an active, enabling government, which seeks to empower citizens and local communities so that they can take control of the decisions which affect their lives.

It is therefore essential that, as I have long argued, we revive Labour's 'libertarian socialist' heritage, which was pioneered by the radical activists of the English Civil War and taken up in the late eighteenth and nineteenth century by the British labour movement as it began to evolve from a series of self-governing societies, groups and institutions – including the early trade unions, friendly societies and the co-operative movement.

This enabling, empowering, devolving socialism – driven by a belief in decentralisation, democracy, popular sovereignty and a refusal to accept that collective action means subjugating individual liberty – is truer to our roots than the statist solutions with which Labour became associated during the course of the last century.

Libertarian socialism has even greater relevance and resonance today as society becomes ever more diverse and the desire for individual autonomy and control grows. Indeed, the variety, complexity and levels of personal accountability which citizens rightly expect from public services can only be fulfilled if we radically rethink what the role of central government should be. Pluralism and local empowerment should be the key tenets of modern socialism, fulfilling Nye Bevan's maxim that 'the purpose of getting power is to give it away'.

We must therefore radically increase the accountability of our democratic institutions: increasing the powers of parliament against the executive; creating a democratically elected Senate in place of a House of Lords rooted in patronage; and making parliament far more representative of the country.

We must also undertake a radical devolution of power from Whitehall to town halls and beyond. While central government must maintain certain key responsibilities – including ensuring high national minimum standards of service provision through progressive taxation – it must also learn to let go and allow local solutions and innovation to flourish, placing a great deal more trust and power in the hands of local councillors.

But wherever possible, power should be exercised by individuals and by the institutions closest to them. I have long advocated stronger neighbourhood democracy – so that, as power is devolved to local councils, it must also be devolved down again to locally accountable neighbourhood structures.

Alongside our effort to disperse and devolve power, we must also redouble our commitment to closing the inequality gap. Tackling inequality, as Tony Crosland suggested, is socialist for the very reason that it promotes 'security, social responsibility and co-operation'. We have halted the rising inequality of the Tory years, but now we need to reverse it.

We must meet our pledge to halve child poverty by 2010-11. Just as proposed new legislation currently requires a Regulatory Impact Assessment, in future we should also have a Poverty Impact Assessment, so as to ensure that all government departments are working towards Labour's overriding goal.

We must also ensure that work truly is a route out of poverty. Equal access to good-quality, reasonably paid, work must be a priority, with more help for those who have moved from welfare to work by providing a universal service which offers personal advice and further access to skills and training and thereby enables them to advance into better paid jobs. And, to ensure that education eases inequalities, we need a great deal more emphasis on supporting vocational qualifications and training, perhaps through new post-16 learning accounts which provide a mix of grants and loans for both academic and vocational study and support.

Our drive against inequality must comprise three other elements. First, the creation of a new Employment Rights Commission, with tough new powers and proper resources, to enforce the work place rights that workers already have and to investigate any breaches. Second, we need to address the rising cost of living – like high utility bills and public transport fares – that hit especially hard those on low incomes.

Third, three-quarters of the extra income created over the last decade has gone to richer households, undermining our efforts to reduce inequality and promote social cohesion. It is time for the leaders of our business community to respond to the legitimate concerns which disproportionate executive pay and City bonuses have provoked by adopting a new culture of corporate social responsibility.

But our commitment to social justice will increasingly face its greatest test with the threat of climate change. As the Stern Review last year underlined, it will be 'the most vulnerable' – at home and abroad – who will suffer both earliest, and most, from the effects of climate change, even though they have contributed least to its causes.

Labour's response must be a new red-green politics, in which the role of international institutions such as the European Union are crucial. We must ensure that the developing world can enjoy increased prosperity without adding to environmental degradation. At home, our red-green agenda should advance radical ideas such as personal carbon allowances, which, by granting equal carbon allowances to everyone, are rooted in the historic socialist commitment to equality and can ensure a powerful, but socially just, response to climate change.

The need for an international effort to tackle climate change highlights the imperatives behind the new progressive internationalism which should rest at the heart of Labour's future foreign policy. In our increasingly interdependent world, the challenges we face at home will be global in both origin and impact. Our foreign policy must therefore be driven by a recognition that common interests and common problems can only be solved by collective action; that global stability depends upon global justice; and that we must maintain the left's historic duty to defend human rights and promote democracy around the world.

Progressive internationalism will mean strengthening and reforming international institutions, such as the United Nations, because only co-ordinated international action can successfully confront challenges, from terrorism to climate change. A reformed UN, stronger regional groupings, and strengthening local civic societies must also be at the heart of our efforts to promote social justice, democracy and human rights around the world.

In all of this, Labour's willingness to show leadership on Europe will become ever more vital. Britain's membership of the European Union makes us stronger, safer, wealthier and greener. At the same time, Labour must show leadership in Europe to ensure that, as a continent, we look outwards to the challenges of advancing global social justice and tackling climate change, and developing a stronger common foreign policy to pursue those and other vital goals. And we must continue to insist on making poverty history, ensuring, in particular, that increases in international aid and debt relief are accompanied by a drive for trade justice, so that poor countries have the ability to trade their way to prosperity.

Real renewal to meet the challenges Britain faces over the next decade is, however, not simply about policy. A progressive Labour agenda is insufficient without a strong and growing Labour Party to campaign for it. Such an agenda is, though, the precondition for that revitalisation. Each will reinforce the other. To reinvigorate our grassroots we must therefore re-engage Party members with policy development, so that every member can be an active participant in the debate on our future agenda, not a passive and disengaged spectator.

But we also need to rebuild Labour into a broad-based party, with a membership that has strong connections to the local communities we serve and an organisational structure which appeals beyond a hardened core to people who are not natural 'joiners' in an era when political parties the world over have had shrinking memberships. And, because it is our connection with millions of working people, we must strengthen, not break, the trade union link.

Labour has never before had the chance to seek a fourth term in government. But we face a resurgent Tory Party currently able to outspend us by a mile, and, above all, with a hunger for power not evident for at least fifteen years. The choice for Labour is not optional: quite simply, we have to reconnect with millions of our fellow citizens to win. If we don't we won't; if we do we will.

Harriet Harman is MP for Camberwell and Peckham and Minister of State in the Department for Constitutional Affairs

PUTTING FAMILIES FIRST

Harriet Harman

A sk about something that happened in the past and women date it by their family events. 'It was after our Sion was born'; 'it was before your dad died'; 'it was when Shane was still with Sandra'.

Most of what we become starts at home; our values and much of our knowledge are learned from our parents, our spouse or partner, from brothers and sisters, or from our children. The family, put simply, is the framework of our lives. It is everything for young children, and as we age it once again increases in importance.

This is not a notion which is – or should be – separate from politics or public policy. Indeed, family policy is key to the Labour Party achieving our aims of equality and opportunity. Though Labour has opened itself up to the importance of family, family policy must stop being a poor relation and become central to economic or social policy.

Family politics must also be very careful and respectful of family autonomy; politicians should take their cues from families, not dictate to them, listening to parents, not lecturing them.

Why families matter to all of us

Families matter to all of us as individuals but they matter to society too. It's at home where you learn to stand up for yourself and to compromise. It's at home where you learn to learn. As Michael Young said, the family is the most important educational institution – more important, even, than school.

Home is where your health is determined and where, throughout your life, you get most of your health care. It provides the bedrock of mental and physical well being. Home is where you should feel secure and learn to value security. Home is where you understand the way generations depend on each other and where you have your strongest connections with the past and the future. It is for these reasons that what matters to families must be at the heart of policy making.

It has taken a long time to get family policy on the mainstream political agenda. I remember when I asked my first question to the Prime Minister in 1982. It was about after school clubs for working mothers in my constituency. In those days you could talk in Parliament about the money supply, motorways and the mines, but my question about my constituents' need for after school clubs was greeted with derision not just from the Tory Government benches, but from our side too. They thought it wasn't politics; that it was a private matter. Now no one questions the importance of after school clubs, just our progress in ensuring they are there for every community.

I can also remember, then, how there was unease and embarrassment about our demands to get the law to tackle domestic violence. Now no-one would disagree with the priority we give within the criminal justice system to tackling domestic violence, or argue that it was a private matter between husband and wife.

And I remember too when, as Shadow Employment Secretary, I developed the policy of a Low Pay Commission to set a National Minimum Wage underpinned by statute, and I argued this as a question of time as well as money. You have to tackle poverty pay, otherwise parents have to work all hours and don't have enough time to care for their children in the way they want. Though the proposal for a statutory minimum wage was bitterly opposed by the Conservative Government and the CBI, the Tories now accept it and the Director General of the CBI who led the attack on us went on to chair the Low Pay Commission.

These issues have migrated from the private sphere onto the public policy agenda, but although Labour in government has made great strides forward, politics in this country has yet to fully recognise something that has always stared us in the face. Every area of policy-making touches families and is influenced by them, so every area of policy making, whether it is social and economic policy, housing or agriculture, environment or criminal justice, must take families into account; how they make the policy work, how they benefit from it, and not just as an afterthought.

The true party of the family?

When I was first elected to Parliament, conventional wisdom had it that the Conservative Party was the party of the family. This came to mean two things. Firstly that Mrs Thatcher's Government wanted to unravel the welfare state and shift the burden back on to women at home. Secondly, as Conservatives, they opposed the change in women's lives which saw women equaling men in educational qualifications and going out to work.

I was advised that I would do best if I steered away from family issues, that this was narrow and I would get myself 'labeled.' However, Labour understood and responded to the change in women's lives and aspirations, and so it was that Labour became the party of the family of the 21st century. With more time off for parents, the National Minimum Wage, the New Deal, massive investment in childcare, education and health services and a stable economy, the election of a Labour Government in 1997 marked a watershed for families.

Now David Cameron is trying to reclaim the family and promising that his Government would 'support marriage'. But it is Labour the policies to tackle poverty and poor housing that help marriage. Remember the saying 'love flies out the window when poverty flies in'. But when a relationship breaks down the Government can help by easing the pain for children. Cameron focuses instead on "sending a message about marriage" with the married couples' tax allowance. But just as the Tories' married man's tax allowance did not halt the trend to cohabitation and relationship breakdown, neither will Cameron's version.

Cameron's new tax allowance proposal would squander public money on those who need it least and carry the unmistakable message to children of separated couples: 'There's something wrong with your family so there's something wrong with you'. And just as this 'message on marriage' will give no help to my constituents in Camberwell and Peckham, nor will it help any Tory MPs who, like so many others, find that their marriages aren't working out. Cameron's policy is nothing more than back to basics – with an open-necked shirt.

For Labour, it's not simply about getting votes off families but delivering for them, with the recognition that the family is the key to our aim to tackle disadvantage and ensure equality in a strong economy and a fair society. The Tories will stop at warm words and will go no further. We have not shrunk from public investment and legislation and we must go further.

The makings of a modern family policy

Family policy today must acknowledge that mothers have entered the workforce and fathers are set to play a bigger role at home. Mothers working help the family budget and fathers' greater role in the daily care of their children strengthens the relationship to the advantage of both child and father. This is why the focus of trade union bargaining has shifted from just getting better wages to include getting flexible conditions that allow men and women to combine work and family responsibilities.

There's been a big change in the age when women start having children and how many they have. For some, later parenthood is a matter of personal choice, but for others it's not a free choice. They delay having a child so they can get a firm foothold in the world of work before they 'risk' having a family. The knock-on effect is profound. It is harder to conceive when you are older, and the demands of work (particularly to pay for the cost of your home) can force you to limit the size of your family. The age of childbirth should be the personal choice of mothers. This is not something that we should allow the labour market to dictate by default.

Parents having fewer children than they want not only represents a personal disappointment for those who want to have a bigger family, it also contributes to the demographic problem of an ageing population and the structural problems this problem brings.

I think we can see more clearly now how families provide the infrastructure on which society and the economy depend. If roads, railways, energy supplies and telecommunications are the hardware, families are the software, without which the hardware is useless.

Making family policy for the 21st century

But like with all areas of government, we must listen as well as lead. Family policy must be designed by and for families themselves. We must listen to what parents say and give them the confidence that we will act.

The Childcare Commission which I chaired in 1999 was based on listening to what parents wanted from childcare and work. *Mothers in Manufacturing* was a report based on what mothers working in the East Midlands leather industry told me about their babies, their parents and their relationships. It was listening to them that underlined to me the importance of getting work patterns right, not just for children and their parents, but also for the parents' relationship. Though we've acted to improve maternity pay, introduce paternity leave and greater flexibility since then, in no small part due to what they said, we still have not done all that we need to do to really let them be the sort of parents they want to be.

Public policy for families will not be right unless it is shaped by families, and currently people see precious little connection between their family and politics. People are familiar with Labour's determination to ensure a strong economy and good hospitals and schools, but family policy is incredibly difficult territory. Any time government broaches the subject, parents feel judged. So, for example, when we press for more childcare for children of working mothers, mothers who are at home with their children feel criticised and mothers who are working feel they are being pressed to work even more, and when we argue for more rights for part-time workers, mothers working full-time feel blamed.

Money

Over the years the pay gap has narrowed, but it's still 12.6 per cent, while the average wage has increased by £2.71 per hour since 1999, the minimum wage has gone up by only £1.45 per hour.

Unequal pay between men and women prevents fathers playing a more active role in their children's early years. It entrenches the division of labour in the home; women have to take time off when the baby is young because the father's pay is better, and this cements the father's exile from the home. She goes out to work less, he works longer to earn more and sees less of the children. Everybody loses.

If we want to ensure that all families can be the key to social mobility and equal opportunity, we have to tackle poverty and we have to tackle unequal pay, and it's because of its importance for family policy that I have proposed that we have compulsory equal pay audits in both the public and private sector, and set a target for ending unequal pay between men and women.

If your family is lower down the income scale you are not only poor in money terms but poorer in terms of time. And when it comes to saving it costs you more. The tragic failure of Farepak showed this all too clearly. Think of those events and activities that family members plan for and do together; weddings, christenings, holidays, Christmas and other religious festivals.

Government could do more to help families save for these shared events by setting up a Family Events Savings Trust. This could support a range of savings plans, including, for example, an 11-month tax-free savings plan, with interest paid at the end, and there could be a top-up for poor families.

This would help families plan and save for the activities they want to do together, and it could offer a practical way of stopping those events, which are such a great source strength for families, becoming a financial booby-trap which undermines them instead of supporting them.

Time

We know only too well that we can't end the pay gap between men and women unless we tackle the issue of time. Nor can we hope to enable fathers to have more time with their children unless we tackle the issue of pay.

It's partly a circular issue, of course. The minimum wage and tax credits have helped greatly, but parents need to be able to fit their work around their family without losing out on better work prospects.

It seems that the more we recognise how important it is to children that both their parents are actively involved in their upbringing, the more parents are under pressure to spend long hours away from their families, earning a living. However, the solution doesn't lie in some kind of throw-back to the 1950s, sending mothers back home from the work place.

I want to see the legal right to request flexible work which Labour introduced, much more strongly entrenched, more widely recognised.

Why don't we put this right into every person's employment contract? We know smoking is bad for your health, so we put a notice on every cigarette packet. We know work flexibility is good for the family, so why don't we require every contract of employment, as well as setting out the details of pay and hours, to set out the employee's right to request flexible work and the employer's obligation to consider it reasonably? Shouldn't all workplace notice boards carry a poster setting this out? Parents should not feel they are on their own trying to struggle to balance work and family.

Flexible work for people with family responsibilities should be vigorously adopted by employers too, because it helps them to build and sustain a committed, skilled and experienced workforce. There is a good business case for this.

Family policy in a parliament of women and men

We need Labour to be confident in its ability to have those discussions with parents and make those decisions, and this has to mean women and men are equally represented. It is unthinkable that a parliamentary debate about, or Cabinet decision on, family policy should be the exclusive province of men. That is one of the many reasons we had to increase the number of Labour women MPs in Parliament and increase the number of women ministers in Government.

The Labour Government since 1997 has done as much as it has on family policy largely because of the influx of women MPs. Quite simply a PLP made up of 97 per cent men (as Parliament was when I joined in 1982) would not have done the job. My view is we would have done none of this had we remained as the Conservative Party still are: a party of men. My concern, as Deputy Leader, would be to put a family focus at the heart of government and to show Labour to be a team of men and women working together. This would reinforce our contrast with the Tories who, although they talk a lot about women in Parliament, have got 179 male MPs and only 17 women – and of those, only three are younger women from the 2005 intake.

It is, however, gratifying to see the Tory men (and indeed women) who over the years have heaped such derision on us, Labour's women, now agreeing with the arguments we have been making for many years.

But Labour's women and men have established Labour as the party of the family in deeds as well as words and we want to do more. To take it to the next stage we now need to create a new connection between parents and politics and put the family at the very centre of all policy.

Alan Johnson is MP for Kingston upon Hull West and Hessle and Secretary of State for Education and Skills

A PROGRESSIVE CENTURY

Alan Johnson

When the Fabians were formed in 1884, England was home to the world's greatest universities. The ideas of our scientists and intellectuals had inspired the industrial, technological and political revolutions that were transforming the world.

Nevertheless the richest nation in the world was also home to the abject poverty and disease that was so vividly described and condemned by the early Fabians. The social progressives who founded the Fabians envisaged a new era of radical reforms covering the constitution, education and welfare.

And yet the 20th century was a Conservative century interrupted by brief interludes of Labour Government. Only in 1997 did we manage to build a coalition of support amongst the disadvantaged and the aspirational, that enabled us to remain in power long enough to shift the political centre ground to the left.

We need to build on the last decade to make the 21st century a century for the progressive Left. This requires five things.

First, we need to maintain the electoral coalition that brought us to power. Those who want to do better for themselves and their family should see Labour as their natural home. We need to show that we can continue to combine economic competence with social justice. In the last ten years, we have banished the notion that Labour wasn't capable of running the economy. We have used economic growth and stability to achieve a more socially just society, tackling poverty and disadvantage, and investing in public services.

Replacing Clause IV rid us of the political dishonesty at the centre of the Party's constitution and helped us separate 'means' from 'ends'. The 'end' is greater equality and the eradication of poverty. Everything else is 'means'.

We know that government agencies are not universally welcomed, sometimes ironically in the areas that need them most. That voluntary sector and social enterprise are often able to be more innovative, more flexible and reach more people than state agencies. But the state remains the only guarantor of decent public services.

Second, greater social mobility must become a major policy objective, ensuring that everyone has the chance to fulfil their potential, irrespective of their background.

In 1997, social justice demanded that we tackle the scars of long term unemployment and benefit dependency fostered by years of Tory neglect. Ten years on, we have virtually eradicated long term unemployment, ensuring that work is properly rewarded with a minimum wage and tax credits, and whilst living standards have increased for everyone, the poorest have seen the biggest improvement. Next we need to tailor welfare provision towards job retention and skills progression as well as job creation.

The hard truth is that social mobility has declined. It is actually getting harder for people to escape poverty and leave the income group, professional banding or social circle of their parents. We need to understand better how governments can raise aspiration. Low parental aspirations in particular are self-fulfilling. We need to ensure that the most disadvantaged groups in society are able to have the same opportunities as the most affluent. Education is the engine of social mobility. Getting five GCSEs increases earning power by a quarter. A university degree adds more than £100,000 to lifetime earnings. As well as continuing to raise standards for all, we need to close the social class gap in educational attainment. This has been my top priority at Education.

Breaking the cycle of disadvantage between generations is complex. We need to start young. Repeated studies show that bright children from poorer households have already begun to fall behind less able children from more affluent backgrounds before their second birthday. Early intervention can halt this trend. Continued investment in early years education and childcare is critical, with the development of Sure Start children's centres central to the project.

Schools need to focus on the progression of every pupil, taking advantage of the detailed information that is now easily available. Extra tuition should no longer be the preserve of more prosperous families. And we need to continue to widen access to Higher Education.

But while education is key to promoting greater social mobility, we also need to recognise the critical importance of other policy areas, in tackling poverty and improving people's life chances. Housing is one of the biggest challenges we face in the coming years. The mismatch between supply and demand constrains labour market mobility and rising house prices have intensified inequality. Demographic, social and economic changes mean we need to increase the supply of social housing ensuring that everyone has access to a decent home. No one can work their way out of poverty without an address; no child can flourish without a warm secure home environment.

Third, supporting families in an ever-changing world. When we came to power there was minimal social protection for working parents, a third of all children were living in poverty and there was virtually no childcare infrastructure. We have transformed maternity and paternity rights, increased childcare provision and established Sure Start children's centres across the country. Our clear dividing line with the Tories is that our family policy is bias-free: we will focus on the welfare of the child, not the marital status of the parents.

We should not, however, shy away from the vital need for parental commitment. Bad parenting has serious public consequences.

Parenting outstrips every other factor, including social class, ethnicity and disability, in its impact on educational attainment. We know that what parents do – reading with their children, instilling good behaviour from an early age – is more important than what they are. Parents will always be responsible for bringing up their children, but children's centres and schools have an important role in engaging them in their children's learning.

Helping parents balance their parental responsibilities with their work commitments must remain high on our agenda. We need to make flexible working a reality for all parents, including those with older children. We must continue to protect our children from exploitative advertising, and recognise that new technologies have some sinister aspects.

Too often our society seems to be at loggerheads with our young people. The Youth Matters strategy invests in positive activities for young people to pursue outside school, through extended schools and community-based activities, so that they have safe places to go and things to do. The power of sport and music to engage the disaffected means we have to do much more in these areas. And our drive to tackle social exclusion must continue, tackling teenage pregnancy and – my personal priority – transforming the life chances of children in care.

Fourth, facing the challenge of globalisation. In 1997 the science on climate change was hotly contested, terrorism was associated with the IRA and China was only just emerging as a modern economy. We are an internationalist party at a time when the major political issues can only be addressed through international solutions.

Climate change is the most obvious example. The challenge for the next decade is to successfully combine multilateral action on the international stage with individual action at the local level. We need to bring other countries with us by setting an example and helping those less developed nations to develop in a way which is sustainable, as well as winning hearts and minds so that we change the habits of ordinary people.

Education is obviously crucial. We can start to change the attitudes of today's generation, but we could completely transform the approach of the next, giving our planet the best possible chance to survive. That's why I want reforms to the national curriculum to give a greater focus to climate change and why I have allocated extra money to make all new secondary schools built in the next three years carbon neutral.

It should be easy for people to make their personal contribution. Installing micro generation in people homes should be straightforward, products should use technology to be more efficient not less (why do we need stand-by lights?), and we should speed up the pace of home insulation.

The increasingly global competition in skills presents a further example. In the past, it was possible for millions of young people to leave school with no qualifications and find work. In the face of increased globalisation, with economic expansion in the East and technological advance in the West, those days are drawing to an end. As Lord Leitch recently pointed out, there will only be around 600,000 unskilled jobs in Britain by 2020, with 40 per cent of jobs requiring graduate qualifications.

That is why it is vital that every young person remains in education or training, full time or part time, in school or college or the work place, until the age of 18.

This historic proposal has been in legislation for most of the past 80 years without being invoked. It was originally included in Foster's 1918 Education Act; then carried into the great Butler reforms of 1944; before finally being revoked by the Tories in 1988. It's now an economic necessity.

This is not about keeping disengaged, disinterested young people behind a desk. It is about making sure that if they take a job it is combined with in-house or day release accredited training so that as well as earning a wage, they are investing in their future.

This prevents them falling into the trap of leaving school at 16 with no qualifications and heading straight into a job with no future. It is this path which leads to the death of aspiration and the corrosion of opportunities for the next generation.

To make this work, we need to make sure that the right sort of education and training options are available. A further expansion of apprenticeships will be central to our plans. Since 1997, the number of apprenticeships has trebled to 250,000. In the future, any young person who wants to take an apprenticeship and reaches the required level of attainment should have a guaranteed place available.

Our new diplomas will provide the missing link in current provision, creating the mix of theoretical and practical education which we've lacked in this country for so long. Their introduction is one of the most radical educational developments taking place anywhere in the world.

Climate change, globalisation, energy security, reform of world trade all require multilateral solutions. It's time to renew our European credentials, burnishing them in the crucial debates on these issues. Only the progressive Left can advance the European cause.

Fifth, rebuilding trust in politics. If we are to succeed in a world of constant change, we need to re-connect with voters in a way that mainstream political parties are increasingly failing to do. While political party membership is down, activism is up. The Make Poverty History campaign involved ten million people.

We should seize the full potential of modern technology, not to replace the doorstep experience, but to replicate it using blogs and chatrooms to promote activism and participation. Our dialogue with voters should be personal and relevant.

These lessons apply inside our Party as well. Being in government makes additional demands on Labour Party members and can leave them feeling distant from the Party they have sustained through bad times and helped elect. We need a root and branch examination of how our members can be more fully engaged in policy formulation.

Our members are the life blood of our organisation so our Party structures must adapt to reflect our diverse membership. We need to attract more people from minority ethnic communities into the Party and remove the barriers that still prevent them from taking representative roles. We need more women in Parliament and in Government.

Restoring trust in politics is fundamentally about the way that politicians conduct themselves collectively and individually. Whilst the profession ranks low in the public's esteem, constituents in the main say they trust their own MP. This suggests that the closer we can get to the electorate, the more they will understand our purpose and respect the political process.

If we are to protect and enhance the opportunities which Labour has spent the last decade constructing, then above all else we need to win a fourth election.

We are now the party of government, and the reason why we weren't for most of the last century was predominantly because of our inability to conduct policy debates in a way that assured the British people that we were interested in their priorities rather than our own.

If we handle this transition with intelligence, sensitivity and good humour, the process itself can be the launchpad for a fourth victory and a magnificent start to the progressive century.

Join Britain's only membership-based think tank

Join the Fabian Society and receive a free copy of 'Narrowing the Gap', worth £9.95, **plus** the Fabian Review environment special issue, **plus** the next two Fabian pamphlets. Call 020 7227 4900 or email us at info@fabian-society.org.uk for more information.

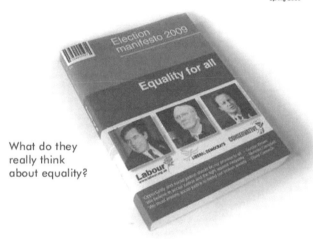

Fabian Review

www.fabians.org.uk
Spring 2006

What do they
really think
about equality?

Inside this special equality issue

Meg Munn and Bob Niven on
Labour's equality programme.

Louise Bamfield asks whether
the Tories have changed.

Jenny Watson predicts a new
alliance of men and women.

Richard Brooks and Sunder
Katwala on life chances.

Stella Creasy on the equality of
local participation.

Melvyn Bragg remembers Phillip
Whitehead's life.

Ed Miliband and Kitty Ussher
recommend equality books.

Tom Hampson sets out Britain's
equality opportunity.

Tired Britain

Michelle Harrison presents
new data revealing the
inequalities of everyday life.

The trickle-up effect

Stewart Lansley on how the
undeserving rich are getting
richer.

The quarterly magazine of the Fabian Society   Volume 118 no 1   £4.95

Featuring: the rise of
the neoprogs

Fabian Review

www.fabians.org.uk   Summer 2006

THE WORLD AFTER BUSH

In this global issue

Sadiq Khan on being a
British Muslim

Jack Straw on increasing
Labour Party membership

Andrew Jones on what's
been achieved since Live 8

Nick Pearce on Francis
Fukuyama's neocons

Hannah Jameson on Joe
Klein's *Politics Lost*

PLUS:
Ed Balls in Gaza

The quarterly magazine of the Fabian Society   Volume 118 no 2   £4.95

Gordon and Hillary
Wishful thinking? Brian Brivati
on the special relationship

Interview:
Paddy Ashdown
returns home

Tom Hampson asks about
Blair, Bush and whatever
happened to 'the Project'?

Nicky Gavron
50 years on from the Clean Air
Act, the Deputy Mayor asks if we
can tackle climate change like
we cleaned up London's smog

The Fabian Essay

*"On a bright, cold day in
January as the Washington
clocks strike twelve, you
might just, if you listen care-
fully, be able to hear a
swooshing sigh of relief as it
travels around the world. As
the 44th President of the
United States takes the oath
of office at noon on the 20th
January 2009, George W
Bush's Presidency will enter
the history books.."*

Read **Sunder Katwala**, p17>>

Fabian Review

www.fabians.org.uk

Autumn 2006

LABOUR CONFERENCE SPECIAL

BRITAIN AFTER BLAIR

SO WHAT NEXT?

JOHN DENHAM
CHARLES CLARKE
DEBORAH MATTINSON
SUNDER KATWALA
ANTHONY GIDDENS
LOUISE BAMFIELD

The Fabian Profile
Can Ségolène save France? The dream of a Royal presidency.

The Fabian Essay
Roy Hattersley on why Labour's next generation need Crosland.

PLUS: Five things our new prime minister needs to know about women voters

The quarterly magazine of the Fabian Society   Volume 118 no 3   £4.95

The Fabian Review, Autumn 2006

FABIAN CONFERENCE SPECIAL

Fabian Review

www.fabians.org.uk

Winter 2006/07

TEN MORE YEARS

BUT WHAT WOULD HAVE TO CHANGE?

The next decade
Five challenging essays on foreign policy, education, life chances, democracy and the environment.

The Fabian Interview
Balancing Westminster and west Yorkshire. A day with Yvette Cooper in Labour's heartland.

The quarterly magazine of the Fabian Society   Volume 118 no 4   £4.95

Fabian Review

www.fabians.org.uk

Spring 2007

THE ENVIRONMENT SPECIAL

GREENING POLITICS

BUT WHICH VISION WILL DO IT?

PETER HAIN
ELLIOT MORLEY
MICHAEL MEACHER
EMILY THORNBERRY
CHRIS HUHNE
TIM SMIT
JEFF ZITRON

What does red-green really mean?
David Miliband sets out his 'next decade' vision of the environment

Progressive or prophet of doom?
Matthew Taylor asks Mayer Hillman whether we can live up to him

PLUS: Women's votes will decide the next general election, says Seema Malhotra

The quarterly magazine of the Fabian Society   Volume 119 no 1   £4.95

The Fabian Review, Spring 2007

Special offer: join the Fabians for just £9.95 and get this book free.

'The Fabians ask the most difficult questions, pushing Labour to make a bold, progressive case on taxation and the abolition of child poverty.'
– Polly Toynbee

How can we make poverty history at home?

One in five children still grows up in poverty in Britain. Yet all the political parties now claim to care about 'social justice'. This report sets a litmus test by which Brown, Cameron and Campbell must be judged.

'Narrowing the Gap' is the final report of the Fabian Commission on Life Chances and Child Poverty, chaired by Lord Victor Adebowale. The Fabian Society is the only think tank with members. Join us and help us put poverty and equality at the centre of the political agenda.

How to break the hospitals' grip on the NHS

In this Fabian pamphlet, **Dr Howard Stoate MP** says that the Government's future NHS vision will fail if they cannot find a compelling public argument which can win locally against the 'save the hospital' brigade.

'Challenging the Citadel: Breaking the hospitals' grip on the NHS' sees health select committee member Dr Stoate and Bryan Jones argue that the NHS is far too focused on the hospital as an institution.

The new NHS should be about public health and health prevention, and if the dominance of the hospitals continues we will find ourselves unable to make substantial improvements in health outcomes, and the NHS will be ill-equipped to cope with the pressures it will face in the 21st century.

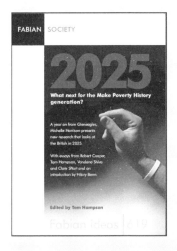

Will the Make Poverty History generation lose its commitment?

Britain came a long way between Live Aid in 1985 and Live 8 in 2005. The Fabian pamphlet '2025: What next for the Make Poverty History generation?', edited by **Tom Hampson**, asks what the next twenty years could hold.

What positive vision for 2025 is needed to keep the British public mobilised? Despite Live 8, individualism is now stronger than community.

For the first time since 1994, according to our Henley data, a majority of people says that looking after ourselves is more important to quality of life than looking after our communities.

Hilary Benn, Robert Cooper, Tom Hampson, Clare Short and **Vandana Shiva** set out their own visions of global change and the politics needed to make them a reality.

The 21st century case for Scotland and Britain

There was a time when saying you were British meant you were probably white and probably a Protestant. But today saying you are British should not indicate the colour of your skin, your creed or culture. It must mean that you believe in fairness, in equality and in social justice.

This spring sees the 300th anniversary of the 1707 Act of Union which created the United Kingdom. As the nations and regions of the world seek greater integration but at the same time strive to retain their distinctive identities, the Act of Union is not a historical curiosity, but a blueprint for international co-operation in the 21st century.

In 'Stronger Together', **Gordon Brown** and **Douglas Alexander** set out powerful arguments in support of the Union and explain why the case is strengthened by the challenges we face, not weakened by them.